Editor

Eric Migliaccio

Managing Editor

Ina Massler Levin, M.A.

Editor-in-Chief

Sharon Coan, M.S. Ed.

Cover Artist

Barb Lorseyedi

Art Coordinator

Kevin Barnes

Product Manager

Phil Garcia

Publishers

Rachelle Cracchiolo, M.S. Ed.
Mary Dupuy Smith, M.S. Ed.

Practice Makes Perfect

Parts of Speech

GRA

Author

Sarah Kartchner Clark, M.A.

Teacher Created Materials, Inc.
6421 Industry Way
Westminster, CA 92683
www.teachercreated.com

ISBN-0-7439-3339-7

©2002 Teacher Created Materials, Inc.
Reprinted, 2003
Made in U.S.A.

Table of Contents

Introduction

The old adage "practice makes perfect" can really hold true for your child and his or her education. The more practice and exposure your child has with concepts being taught in school, the more success he or she is likely to find. For many parents, knowing how to help their children may be frustrating because the resources may not be readily available.

As a parent, it is also difficult to know where to focus your efforts so that the extra practice your child receives at home supports what he or she is learning in school.

This book has been written to help parents and teachers reinforce basic skills with children. *Practice Makes Perfect: Parts of Speech* reviews basic grammar skills for the third and fourth graders. The exercises in this book can be done sequentially or can be taken out of order, as needed.

The following standards or objectives will be met or reinforced by completing the practice pages included in this book. These standards and objectives are similar to the ones required by your state and school district. These standards and objectives are appropriate for third and fourth graders.

- The student uses common and proper nouns.
- The student uses plural, singular, possessive, and collective naming nouns.
- The student uses pronouns and substitutes pronouns for nouns.
- The student uses verbs in written compositions.
- The student uses a wide variety of action verbs.
- The student uses past and present tense verbs.
- The student uses descriptive words and adjectives.
- The student uses indefinite, numerical, and predicate adjectives.
- The student uses words that answer *how*, *when*, *where* and *why* questions.
- The student uses adverbs to make comparisons.
- The student uses prepositions and conjunctions as connecting words.

How to Make the Most of This Book

Here are some useful ideas for making the most of this book:

- Set aside a specific place in your home to work on this book. Keep it neat and tidy, with the necessary materials on hand.
- Set up a certain time of day to work on these practice pages to establish consistency; or look for times in your day or week that are less hectic and conducive to practicing skills.
- Keep all practice sessions with your child positive and constructive. If your child becomes frustrated or tense, set the book aside and look for another time to practice. Forcing your child to perform will not help. Do not use this book as a punishment.
- Help beginning readers with instructions.
- Review the work your child has done.
- Allow the child to use whatever writing instruments he or she prefers. For example, colored pencils can add variety and pleasure to drill work.
- Pay attention to the areas in which your child has the most difficulty. Provide extra guidance and exercises in those areas.
- Look for ways to make real-life application to the skills being reinforced.

Parts of Speech Overview

Use the following guide to help you review the parts of speech that are practiced and drilled in this book. Refer to this overview, as needed, throughout the book.

☞ What Is a Noun?

What is a noun? A noun is a word that is the name of something. A noun is a naming word. Nouns name people, places, and things. Here are some examples of nouns:

> **People:** mother, brother, aunt, doctor, president, baby, teacher, Steven

> **Places:** backyard, house, town, family room, New York, United States

> **Things:** scissors, grass, boat, glove, radio, computer, Statue of Liberty

Nouns can be found everywhere. In fact, you are reading them throughout these sentences. There are different types of nouns. There are common nouns, proper nouns, collective nouns, plural nouns, and possessive nouns.

Common Nouns

Common nouns do not name specific things. They are not capitalized. These are names of everyday people, places, and things.

Proper Nouns

Did you notice that some nouns begin with a capital letter? Nouns beginning with capital letters are called proper nouns. Proper nouns name specific people, places, and things. Proper nouns are always capitalized.

Collective Nouns

Collective nouns are names we use for collections of things (e.g., bundle, bunch, flock, herd, etc.).

Singular and Plural Nouns

Singular nouns refer to one person, place, or thing. *Plural* nouns refer to more than one person, place, or thing.

Possessive Nouns

For possessive nouns, an apostrophe is added to show possession (that something belongs to someone or something).

☞ What Is a Pronoun?

Pronouns are used in place of nouns. Here are some common pronouns: *we, I, you, she, mine, yours, his, hers, its, ours, yours,* and *theirs.*

> *Examples: Jane* is going to kindergarten. *She* is going to kindergarten.

> The pronoun *she* is replacing the noun *Jane.*

Parts of Speech Overview *(cont.)*

☞ What Is a Verb?

Verbs are words that show and express action. They tell the action part of a sentence. There are different types of verbs.

Doing Verbs

Doing verbs are words that express an action, or something that you can see. We use these words a lot when we describe what someone is doing. Some examples are *run, jump, fly, eat,* and *play*.

> *Examples:* The birds *flew* away.
>
> The girls *skipped* together.

Saying Verb

A saying verb is a spoken action. These words are used to describe how someone is saying something. Here are some examples: *said, yelled, stated, suggested*

> *Examples:* They *suggested* we stay here.
>
> They *stated* the rules one more time.

Thinking and Feeling Verbs

With some verbs you can't see the action, but they express action. These are called thinking and feeling verbs.

> *Examples:* I *like* you.
>
> She *understands*.

Being or Having Verb

These verbs are used when something is being described. The being or having verbs are as follows: *is, are, has,* and *have*. Sometimes they are also called helping verbs. They help the verb in the sentence.

> *Examples:* Jonathon *has* the book.
>
> The doctor *is* very good.

Verb Tenses

Verbs also show tense. Some verbs take place now, in the present. They are called *present tense verbs*. Some verbs, however, show an action that has already taken place. These are *past tense verbs,* and they indicate that something has already happened. *Future tense verbs* show what is going to happen in the future.

> *Present Tense:* They *eat* pizza now.
>
> *Past Tense:* They *ate* pizza yesterday.
>
> *Future Tense:* They *will eat* pizza tomorrow.

Parts of Speech Overview *(cont.)*

☛ What Is an Adjective?

Adjectives are describing words. Adjectives describe a noun and give specific information about a noun. For example, look at the two sentences below. The underlined words in the second sentence are adjectives. See how they add more information and description?

Sentence 1: The car stopped.

Sentence 2: The <u>beat up</u>, <u>old</u>, <u>black</u>, and <u>broken</u> car stopped in the <u>dirt</u> road.

Examples: The *nice* lady helped the *old* woman out of the car.

The *playful* dog jumped on her *black* pants.

☛ What Is an Adverb?

An adverb is a word that adds meaning to a verb, an adjective, or another adverb. There are adverbs that show place, time, and manner.

Examples: I told her to drive over *here*. (where, or place)

They arrived at our house *yesterday*. (when, or time)

The baby screamed *loudly*. (how, or manner)

☛ What Is a Preposition?

Prepositions are words we use to show the relationship of a noun or a pronoun to another word in the sentence. They are also called place words, because they tell us where things are. Here are some prepositions: *among, between, in, into, on, beside, under,* and *from*.

Examples: The dog is *on* the roof.

The book is *beside* the telephone.

The plant is *under* the tree.

☛ What Is a Conjunction?

Conjunctions join groups of words or sentences together. Some conjunctions are *and, but, or, when, while, since, though, until, although, unless, because,* and *whether.*

Example: We were able to go to the store, *and* we went to the movies.

6

What Is a Noun?

Nouns are used to name things. Nouns used to name general people, places, or things are called common nouns. Which noun from the box best completes each sentence?

students	beach	bathtub	rat
book	lights	coat	thunderstorms

1. A _____ can be read over and over again.

2. How do you turn on the _____?

3. I love going to visit the _____.

4. The _____ are learning to write in cursive.

5. Only the desert _____ can live in high temperatures.

6. Monsoon season can bring heavy _____.

7. Drain the _____ before you get out.

8. She needed to put on her _____ before she went outside.

Choose the correct name of the noun and write it in the space.

9. The _____ will be open until very late. (**shop, shot**)

10. The _____ from the flower smells pretty. (**pedal, petal**)

11. I brought some _____ from the pound. (**dogs, hogs**)

12. The present was wrapped in pretty red _____. (**piper, paper**)

13. He forgot to touch third _____ when he came in. (**base, space**)

14. The _____ is another means of transportation. (**strain, train**)

15. The _____ is a part of the body. (**river, liver**)

16. The goat chewed off his _____. (**clothes, cloths**)

Common to Proper

Proper nouns are the names of particular people, places, or things. They begin with capital letters. Use the proper nouns in the box to complete the sentences.

Grand Canyon	Christmas	August
California	Veteran's Day	December
Chance	Uncle Mike	Saturn

1. On November 11th, we celebrate _____.

2. Mars, Jupiter, Venus, and _____ are the names of planets.

3. _____ is the hottest month of the year.

4. Sandra missed her flight to _____.

5. My parents are going to pick up _____ at the train station.

6. I am going to leave my dog _____ with the vet over the weekend.

7. When are we going to the _____?

8. Bob's store is opening on _____ 15th in time for _____.

Change the underlined nouns and words to a proper noun in the box.

Andrea	Phoenix	Neptune
Italy	Mrs. Smith	Sunrise School

9. Next week I am planning a trip to <u>the city</u>. _____

10. <u>The school</u> has received many awards of excellence. _____

11. <u>The girl</u> is going to be in the school play. _____

12. Mars, Jupiter, and <u>the other planet</u> are many miles away. _____

13. <u>The teacher</u> gives a spelling test every Friday. _____

14. <u>A country</u> is famous for its pasta dishes. _____

Properly Speaking

Proper nouns are the names of particular people, places, or things. They begin with capital letters. Write the proper noun that best answers the question.

1. What is the last day of the week? _____

2. What city is also known as the Big Apple? _____

3. Where does the president of the United States live? _____

4. What are the four states that begin with 'A'? _____

   _____

5. Who is the president of the United States? _____

6. What is the river that separates Arizona from Nevada? _____

7. What day is Veteran's Day celebrated? _____

8. What is considered by many to be the happiest place on earth? _____

Sort the proper nouns in the box and place under them under the correct headings.

Katy	**Nile River**	**Monopoly**	**Chicago**
United States	**England**	**Mrs. Boone**	**"Star Spangled Banner"**
Matthew	**Joanna**	**Chutes and Ladders**	**Dr. Franklin**
Rubik's Cube	**St. Louis**	**Sesame Street**	

People	**Places**	**Things**
_____	_____	_____
_____	_____	_____
_____	_____	_____
_____	_____	_____

Collective Nouns

Collective nouns are the names we use for collections of things. Choose a collective noun to complete the sentence.

gaggle	cluster	swarm	team
flock	bunch	forest	deck
batch	clump	congregation	herd

1. A _____ of grapes makes a delicious snack.

2. They found a _____ of bees gathered inside the attic.

3. A _____ of birds flew overhead.

4. A _____ of weeds has built up in the garden.

5. The _____ of cattle needs to be moved.

6. They are hoping to preserve the _____ of trees.

7. A _____ of geese can be pretty noisy!

8. He dropped the _____ of cards all over the floor.

9. She cooked up a _____ of cookies for all the girl scouts.

10. There was a large _____ of stars in the north sky tonight.

11. Only six gymnastics will make it on the Olympic _____.

12. The pastor asked the _____ to donate money to the family.

Plural Nouns

Singular nouns refer to one person, place, or thing. Plural nouns refer to more than one person, place, or thing. Select the singular or plural nouns that best fit the sentence.

1. Mrs. Jones has two _____ in her room. (**clock, clocks**)

2. Jennifer bought three _____ (**blouses, blouse**)

3. The storekeeper cut down all the Christmas _____ (**tree, trees**)

4. The girl gave me one _____ on my birthday. (**wish, wishes**)

5. My father cut down all the _____ in front of the house. (**bush, bushes**)

6. I hope at least one of my _____ can go on the trip. (**friend, friends**)

7. The _____ stopped to let me in. (**bus, buses**)

8. There are a lot of _____ in our school. (**class, classes**)

9. The bird flew into the _____ and broke it. (**window, windows**)

10. The _____ broke the gate on his own. (**horse, horses**)

Circle the plural nouns in each sentence. There might be more than one in each sentence.

11. I hope they will open the doors.

12. Where can I find the ornaments in the store?

13. The donkeys kicked open all of the gates.

14. The teachers are teaching the children.

15. The boats began sailing on the ocean.

16. The monkeys broke free from their cages.

Write the plural nouns on the line.

17. one ball, four _____

18. one cat, two _____

19. one man, six _____

20. one window, five _____

Possessive Nouns

Some nouns show possession. An apostrophe is used to show possession. That means something belongs to something or someone. The possessive of a singular noun is formed by adding an apostrophe and an *s* at the end of the word. Rewrite each phrase, using the apostrophe to show possession. The first one has been done for you.

1. the claws of a bear   *the bear's claws* _____

2. the toys of my sister _____

3. the food of the chef _____

4. the papers of the student _____

5. the chain of the door _____

6. the bus of the school _____

Fill in an apostrophe where it is needed to show possession. Rewrite the new word.

7. Sarahs mother will bring the prizes. _____

8. The babys bottle is in the box. _____

9. Marthas clothes were stained red. _____

10. My fathers briefcase is very heavy. _____

11. All of the mans important documents blew away. _____

12. Kathryns mom will bring cupcakes for the party. _____

13. The first graders book has writing on it. _____

14. My brothers shirt is too big for me. _____

Complete each sentence by adding the apostrophe to the noun in parentheses.

15. The _____ homework was eaten by a dog. (**students**)

16. The _____ famous trick requires an apple. (**horses**)

17. Where is the _____ watch? (**ladys**)

18. The _____ ignition wouldn't work. (**cars**)

Categorizing Nouns

There are different types of nouns. There are *common*, *proper*, *plural*, *possessive*, and *collective* nouns. Identify the type of noun underlined in each sentence and check the box in the appropriate column. The first one has been done for you.

#	Sentence	Common	Proper	Plural	Possessive	Collective
1.	The baby's rattle is very noisy.				X	
2.	The children ate all of the cake.					
3.	The Queen of England has arrived.					
4.	His dad is in the armed forces.					
5.	Did you eat the bunch of grapes?					
6.	The lunches are in the basket.					
7.	I heard a flock of geese fly overhead.					
8.	She plucked the petals off one by one.					
9.	We are planning a trip to Las Vegas.					
10.	The horse's tail is tied with ribbons.					
11.	Their family is moving next month.					
12.	Mom told us to clean our room.					

What Is a Pronoun?

Pronouns are words that take the place of a noun. Examples of pronouns are *it, us, they, we, them, her, he, she, him, you,* and *I*. Replace the underlined noun(s) in the story with a pronoun that fits in the sentence. Rewrite the story on the lines below.

Summer is almost here! This means it is time for the club to come to life. Each summer, Molly, Anne, and Elise get the club going again. Setting up a club is exciting and fun. Molly and Anne were the first members of the club. Elise joined soon after. The girls plan fun activities such as hiking, boating, babysitting, serving, swimming, and reading. The club provides the girls with a creative way to spend their summer.

Each member of the club plays an important role. Molly is the leader of the group. Molly believes that her club should be about having fun, but Molly also thinks the club should be about helping others. Molly enjoys organizing fun activities for poor children as well. Molly has the talent of knowing just who to call to get things done.

Anne is good at working behind the scenes. Anne is the one who arranges all of the babysitting jobs. The girls baby sit for free. Anne likes to set up plans to take the kids they baby sit to the park, the beach, and the local library.

Elise adds the energy to the group. When the group members get discouraged or tired of all of their activities, it is Elise's job to give the club members a pep talk and encourage them to keep going. Elise loves to laugh and loves to get others to laugh.

The club is successful because the group members are dedicated and the club offers both fun and service activities. Molly, Anne, and Elise are good examples of what kids can do to make the world a better place, especially in the summer!

_____

_____

_____

_____

_____

_____

_____

_____

_____

Pronoun Preview

Pronouns are words that can take the place of a noun. Circle the pronoun that would best replace the noun in the sentence.

1. The cows ran in the direction of my voice. (**they**, **them**)

2. That backpack belongs to Gretchen. (**she**, **her**)

3. Are they planning to come with our family? (**we**, **us**)

4. Did Suzanne pick up some milk? (**she**, **he**)

5. Michael and Sarah are living with the Adams family. (**they**, **them**)

6. Sadie's mother asked Mr. Frosell if Greg could ride with Frank. (**he**, **him**)

7. The ice-cream cone is dripping all over Elise's arm. (**she**, **her**)

8. Do you think the Smiths are coming over? (**they**, **them**)

9. David, Robert, and Josh will meet you at ten o'clock. (**Them**, **They**)

10. The police officer explained the consequences to our class. (**His**, **He**)

Color each box that contains a pronoun.

she	Matt	it	bird	we
they	page	them	silk	you
their	racing	Yours truly	up	us
he	Sarah	new	young	me
pamphlet	we	I	cat	him
pen	computer	cup	horse	were

Pronoun Mania

I and *me* are both pronouns. Sometimes it is difficult to know when to use *I* or *me*. If in doubt, divide the sentence into two short sentences.

Examples: Susan called Mark. Susan called me.

Susan called Mark and *me.*

Gabby wants a scooter. I want a scooter.

Gabby and *I* want a scooter.

Circle the correct pronoun.

1. Anne and (**I**, **me**) are going to school.

2. Aunt Dixie called Katie and (**I**, **me**) on the phone.

3. Grandma asked Emma and (**I**, **me**) to visit her next summer.

4. Zachary and (**I**, **me**) are the best skateboarders on the block.

5. Mom, Dad, and (**I**, **me**) are driving a new van.

6. Would you like to go into town with (**I**, **me**)?

7. I was sure that Matt and (**I**, **me**) would come in first.

8. Leigh and (**I**, **me**) have been teaching for many years.

9. The baby giraffe looked right at Carol and (**I**, **me**).

10. Between you and (**I**, **me**), I think the principal is right.

11. After school, (**I**, **me**) and Rita are going to the mall.

12. The coach named Greggory and (**I**, **me**) co-MVPs of the football team.

Purely Pronouns

Pronouns take the place of nouns. Add the correct pronoun on each line.

1. These toys belong Samantha. These toys are _____.

2. Does the book belong to Jason? Is the book _____?

3. The goldfish are so pretty. _____ are so pretty.

4. The candy was brought by Mrs. Jeffrey's class.

    The candy was brought by _____.

5. You are responsible for your little brother.

    The responsibility is _____.

Circle the correct pronoun for each sentence.

6. This is the school (**that**, **whose**) won first place.

7. I watched the girl (**who**, **which**) couldn't swim.

8. Is this the boy (**whose**, **who**) saved the girl?

9. Did you help the new student (**who**, **whose**) came from Africa?

10. They are planning to take (**she**, **her**) along on their trip to New York.

11. Do you know (**who**, **whose**) class meets in here at noon?

12. I like a friend (**whose**, **who**) knows my values.

13. Is this the dog (**he**, **who**) does all the neat tricks?

14. We did not know (**which**, **who**) had stolen the money from his coat.

15. The cat was relaxing in the sun and licking (**hims**, **his**) fur slowly.

What is a Verb?

Action verbs express actions we can see. For example, run, walk, and jump are action verbs. Add an action verb to complete each sentence. Use the other words or clues in the sentence to help you find the right verb. Don't forget that you may need to try the past, present, and future tense of the verbs to have them fit in the sentence.

1. Jason was able to _____ the ball that John threw to him.

2. The coyote _____ quickly across the desert.

3. You may _____ when you hear the alarm go off.

4. The horse is _____ his dinner of oats and hay.

5. The rabbit _____ up and down on its hind feet.

6. They are _____ the car around the parking lot.

7. He was _____ her down on purpose.

8. She is planning to _____ every book written by that author.

9. They are _____ off the diving board into the pool.

10. All of the kids were _____ at Seth to stop, but he wouldn't.

Select the action verb in the word box below that fits under each category. There are three action verbs in the box that don't fit any of the categories.

jump	write	listen	skip	swallow
gulp	swing	eat	fight	work
hop	drive	drink	push	read

In the classroom	**On the playground**	**In the cafeteria**
_____	_____	_____
_____	_____	_____
_____	_____	_____

Pick a Verb

In the sentences below, the verbs are underlined. The problem is that the verbs do not make sense in the sentences. In the space below, rewrite each sentence with a verb that you think would fit better in the sentence. The first one has been done for you.

1. The little girl <u>drove</u> the whole way home!

   The little girl cried the whole way home!

2. The dog was <u>painting</u> the pant leg.

   _____

3. The boys were <u>drawing</u> the tree.

   _____

4. Greg and Jenna <u>coughed</u> to the store.

   _____

5. Mrs. Rhoades <u>walked</u> on her lesson plans.

   _____

6. She found a bug <u>sneezing</u> on the table.

   _____

7. The elephant <u>flew</u> by the tree.

   _____

8. A cat was <u>skipping</u> down the street.

   _____

9. Grandpa <u>tickled</u> her shoes for her.

   _____

10. The kids <u>waxed</u> the pizza.

    _____

Helping and Action Verbs

Not all verbs are action verbs. Some verbs are called helping verbs. They help the action verbs do their job. When you put an action verb with a helping verb, they form a team.

Example: The children can read their books.

Action verb: read

Helping verb: can

Complete verb: can read

Other examples of helping verbs are *had, will, is, has, are, am, have,* and *can.*

Find the helping and action verbs in the sentences below. Then fill in the blanks at the bottom of the page by writing the helping and action verbs from the sentences in the correct spaces.

1. Greg will ride his bike to the store for you.

2. Sophia is learning her times tables.

3. The twins are jumping off the bed.

4. Alexis has driven a bike before.

5. We had eaten the cake by the time she returned.

6. They have pushed the door wide open.

7. I am planning to make a trip in June.

8. A motorcycle can race past the mark.

Helping Verbs	**Action Verbs**
_____	_____
_____	_____
_____	_____
_____	_____
_____	_____
_____	_____

Past, Present, and Future

Verbs can tell us specifically when something is taking place. Verbs change their endings to show past, present, and future. If the action is taking place right now, it is called present. If the action has already taken place then it is called past tense. If the action hasn't taken place yet, it is called future tense.

The verbs in these sentences are in present tense. Can you change them to past tense? Rewrite each sentence. The first one has been done for you.

1. I am in fourth grade.

   I was in fourth grade.

2. Mrs. Jones is a well known teacher.

   _____

3. A piano is being sold today.

   _____

4. A dog is a very good pet.

   _____

5. She wants a piece of pie.

   _____

6. He jumps on Monday.

   _____

7. Evan plays basketball.

   _____

8. They enjoy going to the park.

   _____

9. Mr. D's is a good restaurant.

   _____

Verbally Thinking

Each of the following sentences is written in the past tense. Rewrite the sentences changing the verbs to the future tense. The first has been done for you.

1. I enjoyed a game of football after school.

    I will enjoy a game of football after school

2. We arrived at the airport on time.

    _____

3. The teacher was reading a book by J. K. Rowlings.

    _____

4. Susan and Jan competed in the tap dance competition.

    _____

5. The dogs chewed on the shoes.

    _____

On the line, write whether the underlined verb is in the present, past, or future tense.

6. Matthew and Dwight <u>ate</u> at the new restaurant together.   _____

7. Kathryn <u>is coming</u> to the dance right now.   _____

8. We <u>stayed</u> at their house for too long.   _____

9. They <u>will arrive</u> shortly.   _____

10. I <u>am helping</u> my mom after school.   _____

11. Ethan <u>tried</u> out for the play, but didn't make it.   _____

12. She <u>is jumping</u> for joy.   _____

Verbs, Verbs, Verbs

Saying verbs express spoken actions. Some examples of saying verbs are *talk*, *told*, *suggest*, and *said*. Select a saying verb from the box to complete each sentence.

suggested	**tell**	**screamed**	**cheered**	**told**

1. The girls _____ when they saw the mask.

2. Eve's teacher _____ that she consider another option.

3. Ian _____ his parents what he had done wrong.

4. The fans _____ when the team entered the field.

5. I will _____ you tonight when I call you on the phone.

With some verbs you can't see the action, but they express action. These are called *thinking and feeling verbs*.

> *Examples:* I *like* you.
>
> She *understands*.

Select a thinking or feeling verb from the word box that best completes the sentence.

understand	**see**	**believed**	**thinks**	**likes**

6. At least today, she really _____ her new band teacher.

7. I _____ how you must feel after losing your bird.

8. He _____ everyone should ride a bike to school!

9. The kids _____ the story that they were told.

10. I can _____ the importance of informing your parents.

Categorizing Verbs

Verbs are action words. There are different types of verbs. There are present, past, future, helping, saying, thinking and feeling verbs. Identify the whether the verbs are **past**, **present**, or **future** verbs, and write your answer on the line.

1. The ducks <u>waddled</u> over to the bread crumbs. _____

2. The teacher <u>will read</u> us a story after lunch. _____

3. The boys <u>screamed</u> when they heard the noise. _____

4. I <u>walk</u> up the stairs. _____

5. Grandma Jones <u>is</u> ninety eight years old today. _____

Identify the whether the verbs are **thinking and feeling**, **saying**, or **helping** verbs, and write your answer on the line.

6. Mom <u>said</u> it was time to go. _____

7. I <u>love</u> the way the song ends. _____

8. I <u>will tell</u> you after the movie about my day. _____

9. She <u>is</u> running as fast as she can. _____

10. Mike <u>suggested</u> that I bring a friend. _____

What Is an Adjective?

Adjectives are describing words that describe a noun or a pronoun. Complete each sentence by adding the correct describing word from the box.

scary	**raw**	**deep**	**sour**	**light**
melted	**chocolate**	**extinct**	**Thanksgiving**	**gray**

1. I put the check inside the _____ envelope.

2. A sandwich is considered a _____ meal.

3. We had to cook the _____ dinner by ourselves.

4. The intimidating lion had a _____ growl.

5. The _____ meat was in the marinade for hours.

6. She drank the _____ milk for dessert before bedtime.

7. I took a small bite out of the _____ green apple.

8. The _____ chocolate bar got all over my clothes.

9. He dove into the _____ swimming pool.

10. The _____ dinosaurs are fascinating.

Demonstrative and Possessive

Demonstrative adjectives are used to point out which noun is being spoken of.

    Examples: *That* key will open the door.

                  This key belongs to the janitor.

that	**this**	**these**	**those**

Choose demonstrative adjectives from the box to use in each sentence.

1. _____ flowers are mine, but _____ flowers are hers.

2. _____ boxes are already full, but _____ box is not.

3. _____ cat is crazy, but _____ cat is gentle.

4. _____ earrings hurt, but _____ earrings do not.

5. _____ chocolate bar is melted, but _____ one isn't.

Possessive adjectives are used to show ownership.

    Examples: This is *my* doll.

                  This is *your* pen.

Choose possessive adjectives from the box to use in each sentence.

your	**her**	**its**	**their**	**my**	**our**

6. The turtle hid in _____ shell.

7. _____ dad is looking for you.

8. _____ hoe is falling off!

9. _____ family is fun to be around.

10. We welcome you to _____ home.

11. The lizard lost _____ tail.

Amazing Adjectives

Add a *describing* adjective of your own in each space.

Last month a _____ girl and her _____ friend were

driving the mall. On the way to the mall, they saw a _____ car that

was stopped by the side of the road. Inside the car was a _____

woman and her _____ children. The girls knew they should help.

They called the police on the cell phone. Soon after a _____ police

car showed up. A _____ police officer climbed out of the car. He

walked up to the _____ vehicle and asked if help was needed.

Seeing the situation was under control, the _____ girls got back in the

car and headed towards the mall. They felt good because they had helped.

Complete each sentence by adding the best *describing* adjective.

1. The chef sliced the bread with a _____ (**sharp**, **huge**) knife.

2. Last week, a _____ (**young**, **furry**) boy delivered our newspaper.

3. A tiger is considered a _____ (**old**, **wild**) animal.

4. The _____ (**red**, **blue**) apple was cut in fourths.

5. She drank all of the _____ (**chocolate**, **cloudy**) milk.

6. The elevator stopped at the _____ (**attic**, **fifth**) floor.

7. A crab has a _____ (**soft**, **strong**) shell.

8. The _____ (**long**, **soft**) blanket felt so comfortable.

9. An elephant has a _____ (**stubby**, **long**) trunk.

10. The _____ (**flexible**, **pretty**) dancer could move to any position.

Adjectives and Nouns

Adjectives are describing words. They describe nouns and pronouns. Read the passage below and circle all of the adjectives. Then use the adjectives to answer the questions below.

> Early one morning, my hyper dog jumped up on my bed. The bed began moving and my sleepy eyes began to open. Could it possibly be morning already? I rubbed my big, brown eyes and went to get Fido some delicious breakfast. When I went to get Fido's red bowl, he began barking and barking. What on earth? Fido began biting my flannel pajama bottoms trying to take me somewhere. I reluctantly followed Fido to the window. I looked out and saw the big cottonwood tree out front, but that was all I could see. Fido kept barking until I finally opened the front door. Upon opening the front door, I looked down and saw Henrietta, the white, furry poodle from next door on my door step. She gave a little yelp, and Fido dashed out the door. It was going to be a great day!

1. What kind of dog is Fido? _____

2. What color eyes does the person have? _____

3. What color bowl does Fido have? _____

4. What kind of pajamas does the person have? _____

5. What type of tree is in the front yard? _____

6. What does Henrietta look like? _____

7. At which door was Henrietta waiting? _____

8. What type of day was it going to be? _____

Add an adjective of your own to describe each noun.

9. a _____ night

10. a _____ toothbrush

11. a _____ pet

12. an _____ dish

13. a _____ game

14. an _____ tree

What Is an Adverb?

An adverb is a word that describes a verb, and adjective, or another adverb. Adverbs show how something happened. Choose an adverb from the box to complete each sentence.

sweetly	**sadly**	**harshly**	**seldom**	**gently**
slowly	**gracefully**	**quickly**	**happily**	**loudly**

1. The baby cried _____.

2. The lady on crutches walked _____ and was hardly moving.

3. The sun set _____ in the west, and so we missed it!

4. The mean substitute teacher spoke _____ to the students.

5. The boy _____ watched his ice cream fall to the ground.

6. The skater _____ twirled around.

7. Once he was found, Steven _____ joined the rest of the class.

8. She asked her mother as _____ as she could.

9. They _____ come to any of the volleyball games.

10. I _____ picked up the bear cub.

Write sentences of your own that use these adverbs.

11. helpfully

   _____

12. roughly

   _____

13. quietly

   _____

14. sometimes

   _____

15. sweetly

   _____

Adverb Advantages

Adverbs add meaning to verbs, adjectives, and other adverbs. Change the word in parentheses into an adverb to complete each sentence.

1. The teacher reminds them to write _____. (**neat**)

2. The bus came _____ into the bus station. (**slow**)

3. The singer sang _____ on opening night. (**beautiful**)

4. I was sure that I typed _____ enough to meet the deadline. (**quick**)

5. Alison held the trophy _____. (**proud**)

Add an adverb from the word box to the sentences below. Rewrite each sentence.

cheerfully	sloppily	angrily	slowly	hastily

6. The old lady walked.

_____

7. The man jumped off the gate.

_____

8. I listened to the bird whistle.

_____

9. The pig rolled in the mud.

_____

10. She walked over to the principal's office.

_____

Tell Me How

Adverbs answer the questions of *how*, *where*, and *when*. Adverbs add meaning to adjectives, verbs, and other adverbs. Circle the adjective in each sentence. Then, change the adjective into an adverb. Finally, rewrite the sentence with an adverb.

> *Example:* The angry man walked out of the store.
>
> **Adjective:** angry
>
> **Adverb:** angrily
>
> **How, Where, or When?:** How
>
> **Revised Sentence:** The man angrily walked out of the store.

1. The noisy crickets chirped all night.

   Adjective: _____

   Adverb: _____

   How, Where, or When?: _____

   Revised Sentence: _____

2. The hungry children ate in the cafeteria.

   Adjective: _____

   Adverb: _____

   How, Where, or When?: _____

   Revised Sentence: _____

3. The happy teacher smiled as the students walked in the classroom.

   Adjective: _____

   Adverb: _____

   How, Where, or When?: _____

   Revised Sentence: _____

4. The adorable babies played together.

   Adjective: _____

   Adverb: _____

   How, Where, or When?: _____

   Revised Sentence: _____

5. The quick taxi driver left without my suitcase.

   Adjective: _____

   Adverb: _____

   How, Where, or When?: _____

   Revised Sentence: _____

Adjectives and Adverbs

Adverbs add meaning to verbs, adjectives, and other adverbs. Adjectives describe nouns and pronouns. Look at the underlined word in each sentence and write whether it is an adverb or an adjective.

_____ 1. Joanna <u>proudly</u> stood by her parents.

_____ 2. The <u>busy</u> teacher took the time to call their house.

_____ 3. The lady sang the national anthem very <u>loudly</u>.

_____ 4. The <u>dripping</u> rug was hung out to dry.

_____ 5. The <u>terrible</u> accident happened by our house.

_____ 6. I was sure that <u>forgetful</u> Frank would lose his keys again.

_____ 7. Last night a car sped <u>quickly</u> past our house.

_____ 8. Can you please iron my <u>plaid</u> shirt?

_____ 9. The <u>holiday</u> candles glowed in the evening.

_____ 10. The starving animals drank <u>steadily</u>.

_____ 11. The <u>angry</u> wolf showed his teeth.

_____ 12. She was <u>frantically</u> looking for her two children.

32

What Is a Preposition?

A preposition is a word we use to show a relationship between a noun or pronoun to another word. Prepositions can be called place words because they tell us where things are.

Circle the correct preposition in parentheses.

1. Did they yell (**for**, **at**) you for breaking the bathroom door?

2. Timmy wanted to play (**with**, **at**) the elephants in the zoo.

3. The girls sat (**beside**, **before**) their Uncle Johnny.

4. They were all lined up (**from**, **against**) the wall.

5. This story was written (**by**, **from**) the famous author.

Select five prepositions from the box and write a sentence using each one on the lines below.

about	**after**	**beyond**	**by**	**during**	**except**	**into**
near	**off**	**beneath**	**beside**	**up**	**without**	**of**

6. _____

7. _____

8. _____

9. _____

10. _____

Peppy Prepositions

Prepositions tell us the position of things. Choose a place word from the box to complete each sentence. Use the pictures to assist you.

near	on	above	beside	in

1. The duck is _____ the pond.

2. The cow is _____ the rooster.

3. The parrots are _____ each other.

4. The elephant is _____ the grass.

5. The tiger is _____ the jungle.

Preposition Propositions

Prepositions relate one thing to another. They are always followed by a noun or a pronoun. Circle the prepositions. Then complete each of these sentences in your own words.

1. Mom slipped and fell down _____.

2. The girl was behind the car when _____.

3. The bird is on the fence and trying to _____.

4. The child fell off the branch and into the _____.

5. The bike is on his _____.

6. Are you afraid of a tiger and a _____.

7. We went to the movies at the new _____.

8. The frightened kitten scurried under the _____.

9. The pipe is below the ground but _____.

10. They walked right past the cereal _____.

Preposition Hunt

Prepositions show the relationship of a noun or pronoun to another word in the sentence. The noun or pronoun follows the preposition. Use a different preposition to complete each sentence.

1. Run _____ the backyard.

2. Jump _____ the pool.

3. Come _____ me.

4. Sit _____ your brother.

5. Look _____ the igloo!

Change the underlined preposition to a different preposition that would still fit in the sentence.

6. The poodle crawled <u>in</u> her lap.

   The poodle crawled _____ her lap.

7. I looked at the stairs <u>below</u> me.

   I looked at the stairs _____ me.

8. The kids slept <u>beside</u> the tent.

   The kids slept _____ the tent.

9. We rode our bikes <u>to</u> the store.

   We rode our bikes _____ the store.

10. The girls and boys were eating <u>near</u> the kennel.

    The girls and boys were eating _____ the kennel.

What Is a Conjunction?

Conjunctions are joining words. They are used to join words and whole sentences. Choose from the box a conjunction that best completes the sentences.

and	**because**	**if**
or	**until**	**unless**

1. We better wait here _____ my mom comes.

2. I will not forget you _____ I will miss you.

3. The plane cannot takeoff _____ the runway is clear.

4. You will get picked to start the game _____ you practice.

5. Tom yelled at everyone _____ he was having a bad day.

6. We can go to the movies _____ we can stay and watch T.V.

Select a word or group of words from each of the columns to make a sentence. Write the sentence on the lines.

Column I	Column II	Column III
My mother yelled	when	the clown came in.
Jennifer laughed	because	he saw the reason.
Cows eat grass	until	we were in trouble.
Mike wondered why	although	sometimes they eat hay.

_____

_____

_____

_____

Connecting Words

Conjunctions are joining or connecting words. They are used to join words and whole sentences. Circle the conjunctions used in each of the sentences below.

1. Martha could have been a dancer but she had a serious ankle injury.

2. Mr. Rodriguez doesn't know the area very well and we got lost for a whole hour.

3. I was carefully washing the dishes when mom walked through the door.

4. You better hurry or you will miss the school bus for the third time this week.

5. The pet shop has four new puppies since we made a visit to the store.

6. Let's go the park tomorrow unless it begins pouring rain like it did today.

7. I can't wait until tomorrow because we will play kickball in P.E. class.

8. Katie had already chosen vanilla, when Kara chose chocolate.

9. Try to not be afraid of the dark while I am gone tonight.

10. They would sail and fly every day of their vacation.

11. Her uncle lived in the woods but worked in the city.

12. His team had a successful season, although they did not win the championship.

13. She knew she would get better grades if she studied a little harder.

Combining Sentences

Conjunctions are joining words. They are used to join words and whole sentences. When you combine sentences, sometimes you need to take words out or change forms of words to create the new sentences. Read the two sentences. Combine the two sentences into one by joining them with a conjunction.

1. We had dinner. We arrived home.

   _____

2. She got a tardy. Her bus was late.

   _____

3. The students washed their hands. The students ate their lunch.

   _____

4. Dad opened the door. Dad came home.

   _____

5. The flight was late. We still arrived on time.

   _____

6. We were freezing. We got more blankets.

   _____

7. He didn't show up. He was grounded.

   _____

8. She ate her peas. She ate her carrots.

   _____

9. The dog did tricks. The dog ate his dinner.

   _____

10. We had a bath. We were dirty.

   _____

Function of Conjunctions

Conjunctions are joining words. They join words and whole sentences. Sometimes when you use conjunctions to combine sentences, you need to take words out or change word forms, to create the new sentence. Use the words in the box to complete the sentences.

because	**and**	**before**	**when**	**although**

1. My principal came to our class _____ the fire alarm sounded.

2. The police officer helped my sister, my brother, _____ me get up.

3. We won the game _____ our best players were unable to play.

4. We ate a sandwich _____ it was time for lunch.

5. Zachary was unable to lift the log _____ it was so heavy.

Using the words in parentheses, join each pair of sentences to make one sentence.

6. I missed the bus.   I got up late.   **(because)**

   _____

7. The sun is shining overhead.   The storm has passed.   **(because)**

   _____

8. Your collection is neat.   My collection is old.   **(and)**

   _____

9. Sandra cleaned her teeth.   Sandra woke up.   **(when)**

   _____

10. Not everyone got to play.   There was plenty of time.   **(although)**

    _____

Nouns and Verbs

Directions: Look at the following words and fill in the bubble under the words that are common or proper nouns.

1.

over	flies	George Washington	he
a. ◯	b. ◯	c. ◯	d. ◯

2.

inside	stable	running	scurry
a. ◯	b. ◯	c. ◯	d. ◯

3.

idea	before	over	sat
a. ◯	b. ◯	c. ◯	d. ◯

Fill in the bubble under the words that are verbs.

4.

please	stepped	foot	huge
a. ◯	b. ◯	c. ◯	d. ◯

5.

sneezed	on	Principal	before
a. ◯	b. ◯	c. ◯	d. ◯

6.

classroom	is eating	bush	book
a. ◯	b. ◯	c. ◯	d. ◯

7.

sleeping	house	coupon	field
a. ◯	b. ◯	c. ◯	d. ◯

Verbs and Adverbs

Directions: Look at the following sentences and fill in the bubble that shows the verb in the sentence.

1. The monkey climbed the tree.

a. ◯ monkey   b. ◯ climbed   c. ◯ under   d. ◯ tree

2. Our teacher read a story to us.

a. ◯ us   b. ◯ our   c. ◯ read   d. ◯ story

3. The train was leaving the station.

a. ◯ leaving   b. ◯ station   c. ◯ over   d. ◯ the

4. We can open the can with the can opener.

a. ◯ opener   b. ◯ with   c. ◯ open   d. ◯ We

Look at the following sentences and fill in the bubble that shows the adverb in the sentence.

5. A large, brown camel slowly sat down.

a. ◯ camel   b. ◯ slowly   c. ◯ sat   d. ◯ down

6. The kangaroo quickly raced across the field.

a. ◯ field   b. ◯ kangaroo   c. ◯ quickly   d. ◯ raced

7. We happily finished off the pizza.

a. ◯ happily   b. ◯ off   c. ◯ pizza   d. ◯ We

8. They sleepily climbed into bed.

a. ◯ climbed   b. ◯ They   c. ◯ sleepily   d. ◯ bed

Adjectives and Prepositions

Directions: Which word in the sentence is an adjective? Fill in the bubble next to the word that is the adjective in each sentence.

1. The huge door was finally opened.

a. ◯ huge   b. ◯ door   c. ◯ finally   d. ◯ open

2. The gorgeous stars looked down on us.

a. ◯ down   b. ◯ us   c. ◯ gorgeous   d. ◯ stars

3. The final exam was difficult.

a. ◯ exam   b. ◯ difficult   c. ◯ test   d. ◯ was

4. The tired children were sleeping on the floor.

a. ◯ tired   b. ◯ bed   c. ◯ children   d. ◯ floor

5. She brought her new bike to the bike rodeo.

a. ◯ brought   b. ◯ rodeo   c. ◯ new   d. ◯ to

Which word in the sentence is a preposition? Fill in the bubble next to the word that is the preposition in each sentence.

6. The horses are inside the barn.

a. ◯ inside   b. ◯ barn   c. ◯ shut   d. ◯ horses

7. They sat beside one another.

a. ◯ another   b. ◯ beside   c. ◯ They   d. ◯ sat

8. Blake and Lauren are coming after the show.

a. ◯ after   b. ◯ Blake   c. ◯ show   d. ◯ are

Parts of Speech Practice

Directions: Read through the following sentences and identify what the underlined word is. Is it a noun, a verb, pronoun, conjunction, preposition, adverb, or an adjective? Fill in the bubble next to the correct answer.

1. We are going to be late for the <u>train</u>.

   | a. ◯ noun | b. ◯ verb | c. ◯ adjective |

2. The <u>angry</u> man stomped up the stairs.

   | a. ◯ noun | b. ◯ verb | c. ◯ adjective |

3. The <u>new</u> puppy barked happily.

   | a. ◯ noun | b. ◯ verb | c. ◯ adjective |

4. The kids <u>ran</u> when the bell rang.

   | a. ◯ noun | b. ◯ verb | c. ◯ adjective |

5. She was opening the store early that day <u>and</u> planned to leave early.

   | a. ◯ pronoun | b. ◯ adverb | c. ◯ conjunction |

6. The little girl thought <u>she</u> saw a monster.

   | a. ◯ pronoun | b. ◯ adverb | c. ◯ conjunction |

7. The dog yelped <u>noisily</u> as he ran down the street.

   | a. ◯ pronoun | b. ◯ adverb | c. ◯ conjunction |

8. The salesperson called the police <u>after</u> the alarm went off.

   | a. ◯ pronoun | b. ◯ adverb | c. ◯ conjunction |

9. The music played <u>softly</u> in the band room.

   | a. ◯ pronoun | b. ◯ adverb | c. ◯ conjunction |

10. The smiling clowns went to visit the sick children <u>when</u> they came.

    | a. ◯ pronoun | b. ◯ adverb | c. ◯ conjunction |

Answer Key

Page 7
What Is a Noun?

1. book
2. lights
3. beach
4. students
5. rat
6. thunderstorms
7. bathtub
8. coat
9. shop
10. petal
11. dogs
12. paper
13. base
14. train
15. liver
16. clothes

Page 8
Common to Proper

1. Veteran's Day
2. Saturn
3. August
4. California
5. Uncle Mike
6. Chance
7. Grand Canyon
8. December, Christmas
9. Phoenix
10. Sunrise School
11. Andrea
12. Neptune
13. Mrs. Smith
14. Italy

Page 9
Properly Speaking

1. Saturday
2. New York City
3. White House
4. Alabama, Alaska, Arizona, Arkansas
5. President Bush (Answer will vary)
6. Colorado River
7. November 11th
8. Disneyland

People—Katy, Matthew, Joanna, Mrs. Boone, Dr. Franklin
Places—Nile River, England, United States, St. Louis, Chicago
Things—Chutes and Ladders, Sesame Street, "Star Spangled Banner," Rubik's Cube, Monopoly

Page 10
Collective Nouns

1. bunch
2. swarm
3. flock
4. clump
5. herd
6. forest
7. gaggle
8. deck
9. batch
10. cluster
11. team
12. congregation

Page 11
Plural Nouns

1. clocks
2. blouses
3. trees
4. wish
5. bushes
6. friends
7. bus
8. classes
9. window
10. horse
11. doors
12. ornaments
13. donkeys, gates
14. teachers, children
15. boats
16. monkeys, cages
17. balls
18. cats
19. men
20. windows

Page 12
Possessive Nouns

2. my sister's toys
3. chef's food
4. student's papers
5. door's chain
6. school's bus
7. Sarah's
8. baby's
9. Martha's
10. father's
11. man's
12. Kathryn's
13. grader's
14. brother's
15. student's
16. horse's
17. lady's
18. car's

Answer Key (cont.)

Page 13
Categorizing Nouns
1. possessive
2. plural
3. proper
4. common
5. collective
6. plural
7. collective
8. plural
9. proper
10. possessive
11. common
12. proper

Page 14
What Is a Pronoun?
The girls—They
the girls—them
Molly—she
Molly—she
Anne—she
the group members—they
Elise's—her
Elise—she
the club—it

Page 15
Pronoun Preview
1. they
2. her
3. us
4. she
5. them
6. him
7. her
8. they
9. They
10. He
she, it, they, them, we, their, your, you, he, we, me, I, him

Page 16
Pronoun Mania
1. I
2. me
3. me
4. I
5. I
6. me
7. I
8. I
9. me
10. me
11. I
12. me

Page 17
Purely Pronouns
1. hers
2. his
3. They
4. them
5. yours
6. that
7. who
8. who
9. who
10. her
11. whose
12. who
13. who
14. who
15. his

Page 18
What Is a Verb?
(Answers may vary slightly)
1. catch
2. ran
3. jump
4. eating
5. jumped
6. driving
7. pushing
8. read
9. jumping
10. asking
In the classroom—write, read, work, listen
On the playground—jump, hop, skip, swing
In the cafeteria—gulp, swallow, drink, eat
Action verbs that don't fit—drive, fight, push

Page 19
Pick a Verb
Answers will vary.

Page 20
Helping and Action Verbs
Helping Verbs—will, is, are, has, had, have, am, can
Action Verbs—ride, learning, jumping, driven, eaten, pushed, planning, race

Answer Key (cont.)

Page 21
Past, Present, and Future
2. was
3. was
4. was
5. wanted
6. jumped
7. played
8. enjoyed
9. was

Page 22
Verbally Thinking
1. will enjoy
2. will arrive
3. will read
4. will compete
5. will chew
6. past
7. present
8. past
9. future
10. present
11. past
12. present

Page 23
Verbs, Verbs, Verbs
1. screamed
2. suggested
3. told
4. cheered
5. tell
6. likes
7. understand
8. thinks
9. believed
10. see

Page 24
Categorizing Verbs
1. past
2. future
3. past
4. present
5. present
6. saying
7. thinking and feeling
8. saying
9. helping
10. saying

Page 25
What Is an Adjective?
1. gray
2. light
3. Thanksgiving
4. scary
5. raw
6. chocolate
7. sour
8. melted
9. deep
10. extinct

Page 26
Demonstrative and Possessive
1. Those, these
2. These or Those, this
3. That or This, this
4. Those, these
5. That or This, this or that
6. her
7. My
8. Your
9. My
10. our
11. its

Page 27
Amazing Adjectives
Answers will vary for the story.
1. sharp
2. young
3. wild
4. red
5. chocolate
6. fifth
7. strong
8. soft
9. long
10. flexible

Page 28
Adjectives and Nouns
1. hyper
2. brown
3. red
4. flannel
5. cottonwood
6. white and furry
7. front
8. great
9.–14. Answer will vary

Page 29
What Is an Adverb?
1. loudly
2. slowly
3. quickly
4. harshly
5. sadly
6. gracefully
7. happily
8. sweetly
9. seldom
10. gently
11.–15. Answers will vary.

Page 30
Adverb Advantages
1. neatly
2. slowly
3. beautifully
4. quickly
5. proudly
6. slowly
7. hastily
8. cheerfully
9. sloppily
10. angrily

Page 31
Tell Me How
1. noisy
   noisily
   How
   The crickets chirped noisily all night.
2. hungry
   hungrily
   How
   The children ate hungrily in the cafeteria.
3. happy
   happily
   How
   The teacher smiled happily as the students walked in the classoom.
4. adorable
   adorably
   How
   The babies played together adorably.

Answer Key (cont.)

5. quick

quickly

How

The taxi driver left quickly without my suitcase.

Page 32
Adjectives and Adverbs

1. adverb
2. adjective
3. adverb
4. adjective
5. adjective
6. adjective
7. adverb
8. adjective
9. adjective
10. adverb
11. adjective
12. adverb

Page 33
What Is a Proposition?

1. at
2. with
3. beside
4. against
5. by
6.–10. Answers will vary.

Page 34
Peppy Prepositions

1. above
2. beside
3. near
4. on
5. in

Page 35
Preposition Propositions

1. down
2. behind
3. on
4. off, into
5. on
6. of
7. to, at
8. under
9. below
10. past

Page 36
Preposition Hunt

1. in
2. into
3. to
4. beside
5. at
6. into
7. beneath
8. inside
9. past
10. beside

Page 37
What Is a Conjunction?

1. until
2. and
3. unless
4. if
5. because
6. or

Page 38
Connecting Words

1. but
2. and
3. when
4. or
5. since
6. unless
7. because
8. when
9. while
10. and
11. but
12. although
13. if

Page 39
Combining Sentences

Answers will vary. (These are suggestions.)

1. when
2. because
3. before
4. when
5. but
6. so
7. and
8. and
9. then
10. because

Page 40
Function of Conjunctions

1. when
2. and
3. although
4. before
5. because

Page 41
Nouns and Verbs

1. c
2. b
3. a
4. b
5. a
6. b
7. a

Page 42
Verbs and Adverbs

1. b
2. c
3. a
4. c
5. b
6. c
7. a
8. c

Page 43
Adjectives and Prepositions

1. a
2. c
3. b
4. a
5. c
6. a
7. b
8. a

Page 44
Parts-of-Speech Practice

1. a
2. c
3. c
4. b
5. c
6. a
7. b
8. c
9. b
10. c